INDIAN COOKBOOK

DELICIOUS RECIPES OF THE INDIAN TRADITION
FOR BEGINNERS

AKHILA KIMI

2022

Contents

Introduction 7
Spicy Curried Chickpeas 10
Spiced Green Peas Rice 12
Buttered Peas Rice 14
VEGETABLE RECIPES 16
Delicious Spiced Potatoes and Cauliflower 17
Scrumptious Spinach Paneer 19
Tasty Spinach Potato 21
Spicy Eggplant Potatoes 23
Healthy Vegetable Coconut Curry 25
Easy Whole Cauliflower Curry 28
Vegetable Curried Rice 30
Curried Zucchini Eggplant 32
Flavourful Vegetable Korma 34
Potato Okra Curry 36
Delicious Navratan Korma 38
Slow Cooker Sambar 41
Creamy Carrot Squash Soup 43
Yummy Slow Cooked Potatoes 45
Curried Potatoes 47
Mushroom Eggplant Potato Curry 50
Eggplant Chickpea Curry 52
Coconut Eggplant Curry 54
Creamy Cauliflower Soup 56
Delicious Sweet Potato Curry 58
Flavorful Vegetable Curry 61
Delicious Tofu Coconut Curry 63
Creamy Coconut Pumpkin Curry 65
Hearty Potato Curry 67
Mix Vegetable Curry 69
MEAT RECIPES 71
Tasty Chicken Tikka Masala 72

Delicious Chicken Tandoori	75
Peanut Butter Chicken	77
Spicy Chicken Curry	79
Juicy and Tender Goat Curry	81
Delicious Slow Cooked Beef	84
Simple Beef Curry	86
Easy Curried Chicken	88
Chicken Vegetable Curry	90
Spicy Cauliflower Chicken	92
Yummy Butter Chicken	94
Lamb Curry	96
Chicken Quinoa Curry	98
Delicious Chicken Stew	100
Creamy Coconut Chicken Curry	103
Tasty Chicken Kheema	105
Shredded Lamb	107
Yummy Chicken Soup	110
LENTIL RECIPES	113
Healthy Lentil Curry	114
Delicious Black Lentil Curry	116
Lentil Butternut Squash Curry	119
Simple Slow Cooker Lentil	121
Lentil Potato Coconut Curry	123
Spicy Lentil Stew	125
Gluten Free Masala Lentils	127
Flavorful Red Lentils Curry	129
Cauliflower Lentil Curry	132
Delicious Tempered Lentils	134
Lentil Sweet Potato Soup	136
Potato Red Lentil Curry	138
Healthy Spinach Lentils	140
Easy Lentils Rice	142
Lentil Chicken Vegetable Curry	145
Healthy Green Lentil Curry	147
Smokey Lentil Soup	149
Spinach Coconut Lentil Soup	151

Spicy Keema Lentils	154
Creamy Split Pea Curry	156
Lentil Vegetable Soup	158
Delicious Lemon Lentils	161
Tasty Carrot Lentils Soup	163
Lentil Sweet Potato Beans Stew	165
BEANS AND PEAS RECIPES	167
Healthy Chickpeas and Tofu	168
Chickpea Pumpkin Lentil Curry	170
North Indian red Beans	172
Simple Black Eyed Peas	174
Tasty Black Eyed Pea Curry	176
Healthy Green Pea and Cauliflower Korma	178
Red Beans Bowl	180
Chickpea Lentil Chili	183
Red Beans and Lentils	185
Simple Chickpea Curry	187
Pea Chickpea Vegetable Curry	190
Perfect Curried Baked Beans	192
Red Beans with Bell Pepper	194
Spicy Black Eyed Peas	196
Chickpea Coconut Quinoa Curry	198
Red Beans Cabbage Soup	200
Gluten Free Chickpea Curry	202
Vegetarian Chili Bowl	204
Healthy Turmeric Lentil Bean Chili	206
Chickpea Kale Sweet Potato Stew	209
Chickpea Spinach Cauliflower Curry	211
Spicy Winter Chickpeas	213

Introduction

Indian cuisine is loved around the world because of the variety of spices that it uses. Of course, the cuisine is still changing and evolving. The food has become more and more popular which means that the flavors aren't as foreign as they were once before. Dishes like Garam Masala and Haldi are making appearances in kitchens everywhere.

But even as people are falling in love with Indian food, people are running into another issue: time. These dishes are harder to prepare when you are up against the fast-moving pace of the rest of your life. People want to still make good food for their family, but it has to be able to work with their life. Many dishes require much more time and attention than we have to give to the dishes we want to make.

To help you, we're going to focus on the Dum pukht method of cooking. It is a slow cooking process. It means that you'll be cooking some food in its juices. It uses fewer spices but keeps the flavors interesting. And these are dishes that you'll be able to put together and then go off and do everything that you need to do. You'll come home to a house that not only smells great but has a dish ready for you already.

Spicy Curried Chickpeas

Total Time: 6 hours 20 minutes

Serves:

4

- 1.1 lbs chickpeas, rinsed and drained
- 1/2 tsp dried herbs
- 1/2 tsp nutmeg
- 1/2 tsp garam masala
- 1/2 tsp coriander powder
- 1 tsp tomato puree
- 14 oz tomatoes, chopped
- 2 garlic cloves, minced
- 2 onion, chopped
- 1 tsp cumin seeds
- 4 tsp vegetable oil
- 2 bay leaves
- Salt

- Soaked chickpeas in a water for overnight.
- Heat oil in the pan over medium heat.
- Add cumin seeds, garlic, and onion into the pan and sauté for 5 minutes.
- Add tomato paste, tomatoes and spices and sauté for 2 minutes. Transfer pan mixture into the blender and blend until smooth.
- Add chickpeas, bay leaves, and blended puree into the slow cooker and stir well.
- Cover and cook on low for 6 hours.
- Serve with rice and enjoy.

Calories 540, Fat 12.6 g, Carbohydrates 85.7 g, Sugar 18.5 g, Protein 25.8 g, Cholesterol 0 mg

Spiced Green Peas Rice

Total Time: 2 hours 20 minutes

Serves:

6

- 1 cup green peas
- 2 tsp chili powder
- 2 tomatoes, pureed
- 1 tsp turmeric powder
- 2 green chilies, chopped
- 1 tsp cumin seeds
- 1 tbsp vegetable oil
- 2 potatoes, peeled and chopped
- 1 cup basmati rice, rinsed and drained
- 2 cups water

- Add water, rice, and potatoes into the slow cooker.
- Heat oil in the pan over medium heat.

- Add cumin seeds, turmeric, chili powder, tomato puree, green chilies, and salt to the pan and sauté for 2 minutes.
- Transfer pan mixture into the slow cooker and stir well.
- Cover and cook on high for 1 1/2 hours.
- Add green peas and cook for another 30 minutes.
- Serve and enjoy.

Calories 214, Fat 3 g, Carbohydrates 41.8 g, Sugar 3.4 g, Protein 5.3 g, Cholesterol 0 mg

Buttered Peas Rice

Total Time: 2 hours 15 minutes

Serves:

4

1 cup brown rice, uncooked

2 tbsp green onion, sliced

1 cup frozen peas

1 bell pepper, chopped

2 tbsp butter

1 1/4 cup water

Pepper

Salt

- Add all ingredients into the slow cooker and mix well.
- Cover and cook on high for 2 hours.
- Serve and enjoy.

Calories 265, **Fat** 7.2 g, **Carbohydrates** 44.4 g, **Sugar** 3.4 g, **Protein** 6 g, **Cholesterol** 15 mg

VEGETABLE RECIPES

Delicious Spiced Potatoes and Cauliflower

Total Time: 4 hours 15 minutes

Serves:

8

- 1 large cauliflower head, cut into florets
- 1 large potato, peeled and diced
- 1 tsp fresh ginger, grated
- 2 cloves garlic, minced
- 2 jalapeno peppers, sliced
- 1 medium onion, peeled and diced
- 1 medium tomato, diced
- 1 tbsp cumin seeds
- 1 tsp turmeric
- 3 tbsp vegetable oil
- 1 tbsp fresh cilantro, chopped
- 1/4 tsp cayenne pepper
- 1 tbsp garam masala
- 1 tbsp kosher salt

- Add all ingredients except cilantro into the slow cooker and mix well.
- Cover and cook on low for 4 hours.
- Garnish with cilantro and serve.

Calories 123, Fat 5.6 g, Carbohydrates 16.7 g, Sugar 4 g, Protein 3.6 g, Cholesterol 0 mg

Scrumptious Spinach Paneer

Total Time: 5 hours 15 minutes

Serves:

6

- 12 oz paneer cheese
- 8 oz fresh spinach, chopped
- 30 oz frozen spinach, thawed
- 14 oz can coconut milk
- 1/8 tsp cayenne pepper
- 1 tbsp ground cumin
- 1 tbsp ground coriander
- 1 tbsp garam masala
- 1 1/2 cups can tomato sauce
- 3 tbsp fresh ginger, minced
- 4 garlic cloves, chopped
- 1 tsp salt

- Add all ingredients except fresh spinach and paneer into the slow cooker.
- Cover and cook on low for 3 hours.
- Add fresh spinach and cook for 1 hour.
- Using immersion blender blend mixture until smooth.
- Add paneer cheese and cook for 1 hour.
- Serve and enjoy.

Calories 220, Fat 10 g, Carbohydrates 16 g, Sugar 6 g, Protein 20 g, Cholesterol 0 mg

Tasty Spinach Potato

Total Time: 3 hours 15 minutes

Serves:

4

- 1 1/2 lbs potatoes, peel and cut into chunks
- 1/2 lb fresh spinach, chopped
- 1/2 tsp chili powder
- 1/2 tsp garam masala
- 1/2 tsp ground coriander
- 1/2 tsp cumin
- 1 tbsp vegetable oil
- 1/4 cup water
- 1/2 onion, sliced
- Pepper
- Salt

- Add all ingredients into the slow cooker and stir well.
- Cover and cook on low for 3 hours.
- Serve and enjoy.

Calories 168, Fat 3.9 g, Carbohydrates 30.4 g, Sugar 2.8 g, Protein 4.7 g, Cholesterol 0 mg

Spicy Eggplant Potatoes

Total Time: 2 hours 40 minutes

Serves:

8

- 2 medium eggplants, cut into 1-inch cubes
- 1 large potato, peeled and cut into 1/2 inch cubes
- 2 jalapeño chilies, seeded and minced
- 1 tbsp ground cumin
- 1 tbsp chili powder
- 1 medium onion, chopped
- 1 tsp ginger, grated
- 6 garlic cloves, minced
- 1 tbsp garam masala
- 1 tsp turmeric
- 2 tbsp fresh cilantro, chopped
- 1/4 cup vegetable oil
- 1 tbsp kosher salt

- Add all ingredients into the slow cooker and stir well.
- Cover and cook on high for 2 hours.
- Remove lid and cook on low for another 30 minutes.
- Serve and enjoy.

Calories 147, Fat 7.5 g, Carbohydrates 19.4 g, Sugar 5.2 g, Protein 2.9 g, Cholesterol 0 mg

Healthy Vegetable Coconut Curry

Total Time: 4 hours 20 minutes

Serves:

8

- 1/4 cup cilantro, chopped
- 1 cup green peas
- 1 1/2 cups carrots, peeled and cut into strips
- 14 oz can coconut milk
- 1 oz dry onion soup mix
- 2 bell pepper, cut into strips
- 1/2 tsp cayenne pepper
- 1/2 tsp red pepper flakes
- 1 tbsp chili powder
- 2 tbsp flour
- 1/4 cup curry powder
- 5 potatoes, peeled and cut into cubes
- Water as needed

- Add all ingredients into the slow cooker and mix well.
- Cover and cook on low for 4 hours.
- Stir well and serve.

Calories 370, Fat 18.3 g, Carbohydrates 48.8 g, Sugar 5.4 g, Protein 8.2 g, Cholesterol 0 mg

Easy Whole Cauliflower Curry

Total Time: 4 hours 15 minutes

Serves:

4

- 1 large cauliflower head, trimmed
- 2 garlic cloves, sliced
- 1/2 onion, chopped
- 2 small potatoes, quartered
- 1 red pepper, sliced
- For sauce:
- 1/2 tsp cayenne pepper
- 1 tsp cumin
- 2 tbsp curry powder
- 2 cups can coconut milk
- 2 cups vegetable broth

- Add red pepper, potatoes, onion, garlic, and cauliflower into the slow cooker.
- In a bowl, whisk together all sauce ingredients and pour over cauliflower.
- Cover and cook on low for 4 hours.
- About 15 minutes before serving add coconut milk and stir well.
- Serve and enjoy.

Calories 383, Fat 25.8 g, Carbohydrates 34.3 g, Sugar 8.6 g, Protein 11.4 g, Cholesterol 0 mg

Vegetable Curried Rice

Total Time: 4 hours 10 minutes

Serves:

4

- 1 1/2 cups green cabbage, chopped
- 2 cups mushrooms, chopped
- 1 cup broccoli, chopped
- 1 cup brown rice
- 1 tsp curry powder
- 2 tbsp apple cider vinegar
- 1/4 tsp dried thyme
- 1/2 tsp garlic powder
- 1/2 tsp black pepper
- 4 cups vegetable broth
- 1 tsp salt

- Add all ingredients into the slow cooker and mix well.
- Cover and cook on low for 4 hours.
- Using fork fluff the rice.
- Serve and enjoy.

Calories 237, Fat 2.9 g, Carbohydrates 42.1 g, Sugar 2.7 g, Protein 10.7 g, Cholesterol 0 mg

Curried Zucchini Eggplant

Total Time: 4 hours 15 minutes

Serves:

4

- 4 cups zucchini, chopped
- 4 cups eggplant, peeled and chopped
- 1/4 cup vegetable broth
- 15 oz can coconut milk
- 6 oz can tomato paste
- 1/4 tsp cumin
- 1/4 tsp cayenne pepper
- 1 tbsp garam masala
- 1 tbsp curry powder
- 4 garlic cloves, minced
- 1 onion, chopped
- 1 tsp salt

- Add all ingredients into the slow cooker and mix well.
- Cover and cook on low for 4 hours.
- Stir well and serve with rice.

Calories 307, Fat 23.6 g, Carbohydrates 24.3 g, Sugar 10.9 g, Protein 7.2 g, Cholesterol 0 mg

Flavourful Vegetable Korma

Total Time: 5 hours 15 minutes

Serves:

4

- 2 tbsp almond meal
- 1 tbsp red pepper flakes
- 1 tsp garam masala
- 2 tbsp curry powder
- 10 oz coconut milk
- 2 garlic cloves, minced
- 1/2 large onion, chopped
- 1 cup green beans, chopped
- 1/2 cup frozen green peas
- 2 large carrots, chopped
- 1 large cauliflower head, cut into florets
- 1 tsp sea salt

- Add all ingredients into the slow cooker and stir well.
- Cover and cook on high for 5 hours.
- Serve and enjoy.

Calories 295, Fat 19.4 g, Carbohydrates 28.7 g, Sugar 11.8 g, Protein 9.1 g, Cholesterol 0 mg

Potato Okra Curry

Total Time: 3 hours 15 minutes

Serves:

6

- 1 1/2 lbs potatoes, peeled and cut into pieces
- 1 lb okra, cut the ends and sliced
- 2 cups vegetable stock
- 13 oz can coconut milk
- 1 1/2 tbsp curry powder
- 3/4 tsp red pepper flakes
- 2 tsp fresh ginger, grated
- 4 garlic cloves, minced
- 1 large onion, chopped
- 1 1/2 tbsp vegetable oil
- 1 bell pepper, seeded and chopped
- 1 1/2 tsp salt

- Add potatoes, bell pepper, and okra into the slow cooker.
- Heat oil in a pan over medium heat.
- Add garlic, onion, and ginger to the pan and sauté for 5 minutes.
- Remove pan from heat and stir in spices.
- Transfer pan mixture into the slow cooker and stir well.
- Cover and cook on low for 3 hours.

- Stir well and serve with rice.

Calories 290, Fat 17.8 g, Carbohydrates 31.8 g, Sugar 5.3 g, Protein 5.5 g, Cholesterol 0 mg

Delicious Navratan Korma

Total Time: 8 hours 15 minutes

Serves:

4

- 1 cup cauliflower florets
- 1/2 cup tomatoes, diced
- 1/2 cup green peas
- 1 cup carrots, chopped
- 2 tbsp sour cream
- 1/4 cup coconut milk
- 1 tbsp raisins
- 1/4 tsp chili powder
- 1/2 tsp ground coriander
- 1/2 tsp ground turmeric
- 1 tbsp ginger, grated
- 2 tbsp bell pepper, minced
- 1/4 onion, chopped

1/2 cup water

Salt

- Add all ingredients except sour cream into the slow cooker and stir well.
- Cover and cook on low for 8 hours.
- Stir in sour cream and serve with rice.

Calories 118, Fat 5.3 g, Carbohydrates 16.8 g, Sugar 8.8 g, Protein 3.4 g, Cholesterol 3 mg

Slow Cooker Sambar

Total Time: 6 hours 10 minutes

Serves: 2

1/4 cup pink lentils

1 cup water

1/2 tsp tamarind paste

1 tsp sambar powder

4 curry leaves

1/4 cup tomatoes, chopped

1/4 cup eggplants, cut into pieces

1/4 cup pumpkin, cut into pieces

1 medium onion, sliced

1 drumstick, peeled and cut into pieces

Salt

- Add all ingredients into the slow cooker and stir well.
- Cover and cook on low for 6 hours.
- Stir well and serve hot with rice.

Calories 130, Fat 0.6 g, Carbohydrates 24.7 g, Sugar 5.3 g, Protein 7.5 g, Cholesterol 0 mg

Creamy Carrot Squash Soup

Total Time: 6 hours 15 minutes

Serves:

8

- 1 lb butternut squash, peeled and diced
- 1/2 lb carrots, peeled and cut into chunks
- 13.5 oz can coconut milk
- 1/4 tsp ground sage
- 1 tsp pepper
- 1 bay leaf
- 3 cups vegetable broth
- 1 apple, peeled and sliced
- 1 medium onion, diced
- 1 tsp salt

- Add squash, bay leaf, apple, carrots, onion, and broth into the slow cooker.
- Cover and cook on low for 6 hours.
- Discard bay leaf and using immersion blender blend until smooth.
- Add coconut milk, sage, pepper, and salt. Stir well.
- Serve and enjoy.

Calories 163, Fat 11.3 g, Carbohydrates 15.8 g, Sugar 5.1 g, Protein 3.8 g, Cholesterol 0 mg

Yummy Slow Cooked Potatoes

Total Time: 6 hours 15 minutes

Serves:

4

2.2 lbs potatoes, peel and cut into cubes

1/2 tsp chili powder

1/2 tsp cumin

1 1/2 tsp turmeric

1 tsp garam masala

1 tsp ground ginger

1 tsp mustard seeds

4 tomatoes, chopped

1/4 tsp red chili flakes

1 tbsp vegetable oil

1 tsp salt

- In a bowl, mix together chili flakes, chili powder, cumin, turmeric, garam masala, and ginger.
- Heat oil in the pan over medium heat.

- Add mustard seeds into the pan and stir until they start to pop then add onion and sauté until lightly brown.
- Add mixed spices and stir for a minute.
- Add tomatoes and salt and stir for a minute.
- Place potatoes in the slow cooker then pour pan mixture over the potatoes.
- Cover and cook on low for 6 hours.
- Stir well and serve.

Calories 235, Fat 4.4 g, Carbohydrates 45.8 g, Sugar 6.2 g, Protein 5.7 g, Cholesterol 0 mg

Curried Potatoes

Total Time: 6 hours 15 minutes

Serves:

6

- 7 potatoes, washed and cut into chunks
- 2 tsp sugar
- 2 tsp chili powder
- 2 tsp curry powder
- 2 tsp paprika
- 14.5 oz can tomatoes, diced
- 1 tbsp vegetable oil
- 1/2 tsp kosher salt

- Add all ingredients into the slow cooker and stir well.
- Cover and cook on low for 6 hours.
- Serve and enjoy.

Calories 218, Fat 2.9 g, Carbohydrates 45.1 g, Sugar 6.7 g, Protein 5.1 g, Cholesterol 0 mg

Mushroom Eggplant Potato Curry

Total Time: 4 hours 15 minutes

Serves:

6

- 8 mushrooms, quartered
- 1 large eggplant, peeled and cut into 1-inch pieces
- 3 potatoes, peeled and cut into 1/2 inch cubes
- 1 bay leaf
- 2 tsp fresh ginger, grated
- 14 oz can tomatoes, chopped
- 1/2 cup red pepper, chopped
- 1 tsp black pepper
- 1 tbsp ground cumin
- 2 garlic cloves, minced
- 1 large onion, chopped
- 2 tbsp vegetable oil
- 1 tsp lime juice

Salt

- Heat oil in the pan over medium heat.
- Add eggplant to the pan and sauté until lightly brown.
- Transfer eggplant to the slow cooker.
- In the same pan, add onion and sauté for 3 minutes. Add garlic, pepper, and cumin and sauté for a minute.
- Transfer onion mixture to the slow cooker along with remaining all ingredients and stir well.
- Cover and cook on high for 4 hours.
- Stir well and serve.

Calories 173, Fat 5.3 g, Carbohydrates 29.4 g, Sugar 6.7 g, Protein 4.6 g, Cholesterol 0 mg

Eggplant Chickpea Curry

Total Time: 8 hours 40 minutes

Serves:

6

- 15 oz can chickpeas, rinsed and drained
- 1 tbsp fresh ginger, minced
- 2 tsp cumin
- 1 tbsp garam masala
- 1 tbsp curry powder
- 3 cups vegetable broth
- 15 oz can tomatoes
- 4 garlic cloves, minced
- 3 lbs eggplant, diced
- 2 cups onion, diced
- 2 tsp salt

- Add all ingredients except chickpeas into the slow cooker.
- Cover and cook on low for 8 hours.
- Add chickpeas and cook for another 30 minutes.
- Stir well and serve.

Calories 203, Fat 2.3 g, Carbohydrates 39.2 g, Sugar 11.3 g, Protein 9.7 g, Cholesterol 0 mg

Coconut Eggplant Curry

Total Time: 4 hours 10 minutes

Serves:

6

- 2 lbs eggplant, cut into 1 inch cubed
- 4 garlic cloves, minced
- 14.5 oz can coconut milk
- 6 oz tomato paste
- 1 tbsp curry powder
- 1 medium onion, chopped
- 1 green bell pepper, seeded and chopped
- 2 Serrano peppers, seeded and minced
- 1 tbsp garam masala
- 1 tsp salt

- Add all ingredients into the slow cooker and stir well.
- Cover and cook on low for 4 hours.
- Serve and enjoy.

Calories 216, Fat 15.2 g, Carbohydrates 20.7 g, Sugar 9.8 g, Protein 4.8 g, Cholesterol 0 mg

Creamy Cauliflower Soup

Total Time: 4 hours 20 minutes

Serves:

6

- 1 cauliflower head
- 2 cups vegetable broth
- 3 garlic cloves
- 1/4 cup dried cranberries
- 1/4 cup pine nuts
- 13.5 oz can coconut milk
- 5.3 oz plain yogurt
- 1 tbsp curry powder
- 1 tbsp water
- 3/4 tsp garam masala
- 1/2 cup sugar
- 1/2 tsp salt

- Add cauliflower, broth, and garlic into the slow cooker. Cover and cook on low for 4 hours.
- Add cauliflower mixture into the blender along with yogurt and coconut milk and blend until smooth.
- Pour into the six serving bowls.
- In a pan, cook over medium heat pine nuts with water, garam masala, and sugar. Cook until sugar is crystallized.
- Sprinkle pan mixture over the soup.
- Serve and enjoy.

Calories 276, Fat 18.5 g, Carbohydrates 25.1 g, Sugar 20.1 g, Protein 6.2 g, Cholesterol 2 mg

Delicious Sweet Potato Curry

Total Time: 6 hours 15 minutes

Serves:

6

- 1 sweet potato, diced
- 1 courgette, diced
- 1/4 cup cashew nuts
- 14 oz can tomatoes, chopped
- 1 tsp curry powder
- 1/2 tsp chili powder
- 1/2 tsp black pepper
- 2 tbsp tomato puree
- 4 tbsp flour
- 14 oz can coconut milk
- 1 tsp garlic, minced
- 2 onions, diced
- 4 tomatoes, diced
- 1 tsp ginger, minced
- 2 tsp garam masala
- 1 tbsp vegetable oil

- Heat oil in the pan over medium heat.
- Add ginger, onion, and garlic to the pan and sauté for 5 minutes.
- Add tomato paste, flour, and spices and cook for a minute.
- Add coconut milk and stir well and cook until thickened.
- Transfer pan mixture into the slow cooker along with remaining ingredients and mix well.
- Cover and cook on low for 6 hours.
- Serve and enjoy.

Calories 275, Fat 19.5 g, Carbohydrates 24 g, Sugar 8.3 g, Protein 5.5 g, Cholesterol 0 mg

Flavorful Vegetable Curry

Total Time: 7 hours 15 minutes

Serves:

4

- 15 oz can chickpeas, rinsed and drained
- 8 oz fresh green beans, cut into 1-inch pieces
- 4 medium carrots, sliced
- 2 medium potatoes, cut into 1/2 inch cubes
- 1 cup onion, chopped
- 14 oz can vegetable broth
- 14 oz can tomatoes, diced
- 2 tbsp tapioca
- 2 tsp curry powder
- 1 tsp ground coriander
- 3 garlic cloves, minced
- 1/8 tsp ground cinnamon
- 1/4 tsp red pepper, crushed
- 1/4 tsp salt

- Add all ingredients into the slow cooker and stir well.
- Cover and cook on low for 7 hours.
- Stir well and serve with rice.

Calories 367, Fat 3.1 g, Carbohydrates 75.3 g Sugar 11.8 g, Protein 12.6 g, Cholesterol 1 mg

Delicious Tofu Coconut Curry

Total Time: 4 hours 15 minutes

Serves: 4

- 1 cup firm tofu, diced
- 2 tsp garlic cloves, minced
- 1 cup onion, chopped
- 8 oz tomato paste
- 2 cups bell pepper, chopped
- 1 tbsp garam masala
- 2 tbsp butter
- 1 tbsp curry powder
- 10 oz can coconut milk
- 1 1/2 tsp sea salt

- Add all ingredients into the slow cooker and stir well.
- Cover and cook on low for 4 hours.
- Stir well and serve with rice.

Calories 179, Fat 9.1 g, Carbohydrates 20.4 g, Sugar 11.6 g, Protein 8.9 g, Cholesterol 15 mg

Creamy Coconut Pumpkin Curry

Total Time: 6 hours 15 minutes

Serves:

6

---

15 oz can coconut milk, unsweetened

2 cups pumpkin puree

1 cup vegetable stock

3 carrots, cut into 1-inch pieces

3 cups sweet potatoes, cut into 1-inch cubes

1/2 tbsp curry powder

1/4 tsp turmeric powder

1/4 tsp ground black pepper

1/2 large onion, diced

1 garlic clove, minced

2 chicken breasts, cut into 1-inch cubes

1 lime juice

2 tsp garam masala

1/2 tsp kosher salt

- Add all ingredients into the slow cooker and mix well.
- Cover and cook on low for 6 hours.
- Serve with rice and enjoy.

Calories 357, Fat 17.7 g, Carbohydrates 35 g, Sugar 7.4 g, Protein 17.6 g, Cholesterol 43 mg

Hearty Potato Curry

Total Time: 8 hours 10 minutes

Serves:

4

- 1 lb potatoes, cut into 1-inch cubes
- 1/2 tsp cumin
- 1/2 tsp coriander
- 1/2 tsp peppercorns
- 1 cinnamon stick
- 1 cups vegetable stock
- 1 tsp tamarind paste
- 1 bay leaf
- 1/4 tsp red pepper, crushed
- 1/2 tsp garam masala
- 4 garlic cloves, minced
- 2 tsp ginger, minced
- 1 onion, diced
- 2 tbsp vegetable oil
- 1 1/2 tsp paprika

1 1/2 tsp turmeric

1/2 cup frozen peas

2 cups coconut milk

2 tbsp all purpose flour

Pepper

Salt

- Heat 1 tbsp oil in the pan over medium heat.
- Add onion and cook until golden brown, about 3 minutes.
- Add powder spices and stir for 1 minute.
- Transfer onion mixture to the blender with tamarind, ginger, garlic, and coconut milk and blend until smooth.
- Pour blended mixture into the slow cooker with remaining ingredients except for peas and flour.
- Cover and cook on low for 8 hours.
- Add peas and stir well. Whisk flour in little water and pour into the slow cooker.
- Stir well and serve.

Calories 476, Fat 36.5 g, Carbohydrates 37.2 g, Sugar 8.8 g, Protein 7 g, Cholesterol 0 mg

Mix Vegetable Curry

Total Time: 6 hours 10 minutes

Serves: 4

- 3 1/2 cups broccoli florets
- 2.5 oz green beans
- 2 medium carrots, peeled and sliced
- 2 large sweet potatoes, diced
- 3 tbsp tomato puree
- 14 oz can coconut milk
- 1 red chili, seeded and chopped
- 1 tsp garam masala
- 1 tsp ground turmeric
- 2 tsp ground coriander
- 2 tsp ground cumin
- 1 tsp chili powder
- 1 tsp ginger, grated
- 1 tsp garlic, grated
- 1 onion, diced

- Add all ingredients except green beans into the slow cooker and mix well.
- Cover and cook on low for 5 hours.
- Add green beans and stir well and cook for another 1 hour.
- Serve with rice.

Calories 313, Fat 22 g, Carbohydrates 28.3 g, Sugar 5.1 g, Protein 6.3 g, Cholesterol 0 mg

MEAT RECIPES

Tasty Chicken Tikka Masala

Total Time: 6 hours 25 minutes

Serves:

6

2 lbs chicken thighs, skinless and boneless, cut into 2-inch pieces

10 oz frozen peas, thawed

1 1/2 cups heavy cream

1 tbsp cornstarch

1 tbsp sugar

28 oz can tomatoes

1 tsp ginger, grated

3 tbsp garam masala

1/2 tsp red pepper flakes

6 garlic cloves, minced

1 large onion, diced

2 tbsp vegetable oil

1 cup plain yogurt

1 tbsp ground cumin

1 tbsp ground coriander

1 tsp kosher salt

- In a large bowl, combine together chicken, yogurt, cumin, ground coriander, and salt. Marinade for 10 minutes.
- Heat 1 tbsp oil in the pan over medium-high heat.
- Place marinated chicken into the pan and cook until lightly brown on both the sides.
- Transfer chicken into the slow cooker.
- In the same pan, heat remaining oil. Add onions, red pepper flakes, and garlic and saute for 5 minutes.
- Add ginger, garam masala, and salt and cook for 1 minute.
- Add sugar and tomatoes, turn heat to high and bring to boil. Transfer into the slow cooker.
- Cover and cook on low for 6 hours.
- Whisk together 1/4 cup heavy cream and cornstarch and add to the slow cooker along with remaining peas and heavy cream.
- Stir to mix and cover and cook for another 10 minutes.
- Serve and enjoy.

Calories 557, Fat 27.8 g, Carbohydrates 24.5 g, Sugar 12.7 g, Protein 51.1 g, Cholesterol 178 mg

Delicious Chicken Tandoori

Total Time: 8 hours 20 minutes

Serves:

4

- 14 oz coconut milk
- 4 chicken thighs
- 1 tsp fresh ginger, grated
- 1 tsp paprika
- 1 tsp cayenne pepper
- 2 tsp tomato paste
- 2 tsp garam masala
- 1 tsp ground coriander
- 1 tsp ground cumin

- Add all ingredients into the slow cooker and mix well.
- Cover and cook on low for 8 hours.
- Serve and enjoy.

Calories 514, Fat 34.8 g, Carbohydrates 7.1 g, Sugar 3.8 g, Protein 44.9 g, Cholesterol 130 mg

Peanut Butter Chicken

Total Time: 4 hours 30 minutes

Serves:

6

- 3 chicken breasts, skinless and boneless
- 1 tbsp lime juice
- 2 tbsp cornstarch
- 3 garlic cloves, minced
- 1 tbsp ginger, minced
- 1 tbsp rice wine vinegar
- 2 tbsp honey
- 2 tbsp soy sauce
- 1/3 cup creamy peanut butter
- 1 cup coconut milk

- Add all ingredients except lime juice and cornstarch into the slow cooker and mix well.
- Cover and cook on low for 4 hours.
- Whisk together cornstarch and 2 tbsp water and pour into the slow cooker.
- Stir well and cook for another 20 minutes until gravy thickens.
- Serve and enjoy.

Calories 356, Fat 22.2 g, Carbohydrates 15.4 g, Sugar 8.7 g, Protein 26.2 g, Cholesterol 65 mg

Spicy Chicken Curry

Total Time: 6 hours 20 minutes

Serves:

4

- 4 chicken thighs, boneless and cut into chunks
- 3 tbsp flour
- 2 tsp ground coriander
- 2 tsp garam masala
- 2 tsp turmeric
- 2 tsp ground cumin
- 1 tsp ginger, grated
- 1/2 lemon juice
- 4 garlic cloves, crushed
- 2 onion, chopped
- 2 green chilies, chopped
- 14 oz can tomatoes, chopped
- 1 tbsp vegetable oil

- Add ginger, chilies, garlic, and onion into the blender and blend until smooth.
- Heat oil in the pan over medium heat.
- Add blended puree into the pan and sauté for 3 minutes.
- Add spices and sauté for 2-3 minutes.
- Add flour and tomatoes into the pan and stir well.
- Refill tomato can halfway with water and adds in the pan. Stir well.
- Add chicken into the slow cooker and season with pepper and salt.
- Pour pan mixture over the chicken with lemon juice.
- Cover and cook on low for 6 hours.
- Serve and enjoy.

Calories 387, Fat 14.8 g, Carbohydrates 17.3 g, Sugar 6 g, Protein 44.9 g, Cholesterol 130 mg

Juicy and Tender Goat Curry

Total Time: 5 hours 15 minutes

Serves:

6

- 2 lbs goat meat
- 2 Serrano pepper, minced
- 1 tsp paprika
- 1 tsp chili powder
- 1 tsp turmeric powder
- 1 tsp cumin powder
- 1 tbsp coriander powder
- 2 cardamom pods
- 2 garlic cloves, minced
- 1 tbsp ghee
- 1 bay leaf
- 3 whole cloves
- 1 tsp fresh ginger, minced

1 large onion, chopped

1 cup water

1 tsp garam masala

28 oz can tomatoes, diced

2 tsp salt

- Add cardamom and cloves into the grinder and grind well.
- Add all ingredients into the slow cooker except water, garam masala, and tomatoes.
- Cover and cook on high for 4 hours.
- Add water, garam masala, and tomatoes and stir well.
- Cook for another 1 hour until meat is tender.

- Serve and enjoy.

Calories 230, Fat 5.9 g, Carbohydrates 10.6 g, Sugar 5.8 g, Protein 33.6 g, Cholesterol 92 mg

Delicious Slow Cooked Beef

Total Time: 6 hours 15 minutes

Serves:

4

- 2 lbs beef chuck steak, diced
- 1/2 cup coriander, chopped
- 2 cardamom pods
- 1 cinnamon stick
- 14 oz can tomatoes, diced
- 1/4 cup curry paste
- 1 red chili, chopped
- 1 tsp ginger, grated
- 2 garlic cloves, crushed
- 1 large onion, sliced
- 2 tbsp vegetable oil
- 1/4 cup plain flour

- Add beef and flour into the ziplock bag and shake well.
- Heat oil in the saucepan over medium heat.
- Add beef into the saucepan and cook for 3-4 minutes or until lightly brown. Transfer beef into the slow cooker.
- In the same pan, add onion, ginger, and garlic and sauté for 4 minutes.
- Add curry paste and chili and stir for 1 minute.
- Add 3/4 cup water, tomatoes, cardamom, and cinnamon and stir well. Transfer mixture into the slow cooker.
- Cover and cook on low for 5 1/2 hours or until beef is tender.
- Add coriander and stir well.
- Serve and enjoy.

Calories 651, Fat 29.9 g, Carbohydrates 19.7 g, Sugar 5 g, Protein 71.8 g, Cholesterol 203 mg

Simple Beef Curry

Total Time: 8 hours 40 minutes

Serves:

4

- 12 oz beef steak, cut into 1-inch pieces
- 2 onions, chopped
- 14 oz can tomatoes, chopped
- 2 tsp garam masala
- 4 garlic cloves, chopped
- 4 tsp ground cumin
- 4 tsp ground coriander
- 2 tsp ground turmeric
- 2 chilies, chopped
- 1 tsp ginger, grated
- 7 oz yogurt
- 4 tbsp vegetable oil

- Heat oil in the pan over medium heat.
- Add beef to the pan and cook for 4-5 minutes or until lightly brown. Transfer beef into the slow cooker.
- In the same pan, sauté onion, ginger, chili, and garlic for 2 minutes.
- Add spices and stir-fry for 1 minute. Transfer pan mixture to the slow cooker.
- Add remaining ingredients except for yogurt into the slow cooker and stir well.
- Cover and cook on low for 8 hours.
- Add yogurt and stir well and cook for another 30 minutes.
- Serve and enjoy.

Calories 375, Fat 20.2 g, Carbohydrates 16.7 g, Sugar 9.3 g, Protein 30.8 g, Cholesterol 79 mg

Easy Curried Chicken

Total Time: 4 hours 15 minutes

Serves:

4

- 2 tbsp tomato paste
- 14 oz can coconut milk
- 3 garlic cloves, minced
- 2 tbsp fresh ginger, minced
- 1 tsp cumin
- 1 tsp turmeric
- 1 tsp garam masala
- 1 cinnamon stick
- 2 bay leaves
- 1 1/2 lbs chicken thighs
- 1 medium onion, diced
- 1/4 cup fresh cilantro, chopped
- 1 1/2 tsp salt

- Add all ingredients into the slow cooker and stir well.
- Cover and cook on low for 4 hours.
- Using fork shred the meat and stir well into the sauce.
- Serve and enjoy.

Calories 553, Fat 34.2 g, Carbohydrates 10.2 g, Sugar 2.3 g, Protein 52.4 g, Cholesterol 151 mg

Chicken Vegetable Curry

Total Time: 3 hours 25 minutes

Serves:

4

- 2 cups mushrooms, sliced
- 1 cup green peas
- 3 chicken breasts, skinless, boneless and cut into pieces
- 2 tsp ground cayenne
- 1/2 tsp black pepper
- 3 tbsp curry powder
- 1 packet dry onion soup mix
- 14 oz can coconut milk
- 10.75 oz can chicken soup
- 10.75 oz can mushroom soup
- 1 onion, chopped
- 1 tbsp butter

- Melt butter in the pan over medium heat.
- Add onion and cook for 5 minutes. Transfer to the slow cooker.
- Add remaining ingredients and stir well.
- Cover and cook on high for 1 1/2 hours then reduce heat to low and cook for another 1 1/2 hours.
- Serve and enjoy.

Calories 635, Fat 37.9 g, Carbohydrates 32 g, Sugar 2.3 g, Protein 45.2 g, Cholesterol 111 mg

Spicy Cauliflower Chicken

Total Time: 6 hours 15 minutes

Serves:
4

- 1 1/2 lbs chicken thighs, skinless, boneless and cut into halves
- 1 small cauliflower head, cut into florets
- 1/4 cup raisins
- 1 onion, chopped
- 1 tbsp curry powder
- 2 tbsp ginger, grated
- 2 tbsp tomato paste
- 28 oz can tomatoes, diced
- 1/2 tsp kosher salt

- Add all ingredients into the slow cooker and stir well.
- Cover and cook on low for 6 hours.
- Serve and enjoy.

Calories 391, Fat 17.3 g, Carbohydrates 26.7 g, Sugar 6.7 g, Protein 31.1 g, Cholesterol 96 mg

Yummy Butter Chicken

Total Time: 4 hours 30 minutes

Serves:

6

---

4 large chicken thighs, skinless, boneless and cut into pieces

14 oz can coconut milk

1 cup plain yogurt

15 green cardamom pods

6 oz can tomato paste

1 tsp garam masala

2 tsp tandoori masala

1 tsp curry paste

2 tsp curry powder

3 garlic cloves, minced

1 onion, diced

3 tbsp vegetable oil

2 tbsp butter

Salt

- Heat butter and oil in a pan over medium heat.
- Add chicken, garlic, and onion to the pan and cook until onion softens.
- Stir in tomato paste, garam masala, tandoori masala, curry paste, and curry powder.
- Transfer chicken mixture into the slow cooker.
- Stir in yogurt, coconut milk, and cardamom pods.
- Season with salt.
- Cover and cook on high for 4 hours.
- Serve and enjoy.

Calories 480, Fat 33.3 g, Carbohydrates 17.2 g, Sugar 7.1 g, Protein 30.6 g, Cholesterol 103 mg

Lamb Curry

Total Time: 8 hours 15 minutes

Serves:

6

- 2 lbs lamb meat, cut into 1 1/2" cubes
- 1/4 cup cilantro, chopped
- 20 almonds
- 1/4 tsp saffron threads
- 1 cup plain yogurt
- 1/2 tsp turmeric
- 2 large onion, sliced
- 6 tbsp vegetable oil
- 3 tomatoes, chopped
- 1/4 cup dried coconut, unsweetened
- 5 garlic cloves, crushed
- 1 tsp fresh ginger, grated
- 1 tsp garam masala
- 1 tsp cumin seeds
- 3 green Chile pepper

4 dried red Chile pepper

Salt

- Add tomatoes, grated coconut, garlic, ginger, garam masala, cumin seeds, green chilies, and red chilies into the blender and blend until smooth.
- Heat oil in a pan over medium heat.
- Add onion to the pan and sauté for 5 minutes or until softened.
- Add spice paste to the pan and cook for 3 minutes.
- Stir in meat and salt. Cook over medium heat for 8 minutes.
- Mix in almonds, saffron, and yogurt until well combined.
- Transfer pan mixture into the slow cooker and stir well.
- Cover and cook on low for 8 hours.
- Serve and enjoy.

Calories 489, Fat 35.4 g, Carbohydrates 16.1 g, Sugar 7.1 g, Protein 28.1 g, Cholesterol 88 mg

Chicken Quinoa Curry

Total Time: 4 hours 45 minutes

Serves:

6

- 1 1/2 lbs chicken breast, diced
- 1/3 cup quinoa
- 1/4 tsp paprika
- 1 tbsp curry powder
- 1/4 cup coconut milk
- 1 cup chicken broth
- 1 3/4 cups apples, chopped
- 1 1/4 cups celery, chopped
- 3/4 cup onion, chopped

- Add all ingredients except quinoa into the slow cooker and stir well.
- Cover and cook on low for 4 hours.
- Add quinoa and stir well. Cook for another 35 minutes.
- Stir well and serve.

Calories 185, Fat 3.1 g, Carbohydrates 14.4 g, Sugar 8.2 g, Protein 24.4 g, Cholesterol 59 mg

Delicious Chicken Stew

Total Time: 4 hours 15 minutes

Serves:

8

- 2 lbs chicken thighs, skinless, boneless and cut into pieces
- 1 medium onion, chopped
- 3 garlic cloves, minced
- 1/4 tsp ground black pepper
- 15 oz can chickpeas, rinsed and drained
- 14 oz can tomatoes, diced
- 1 cup chicken broth
- 5 tsp curry powder
- 2 tsp ground ginger
- 1 bay leaf
- 1 tbsp vegetable oil
- 2 tbsp lime juice
- 1/2 tsp salt

- Add all ingredients into the slow cooker and mix well.
- Cover and cook on high for 4 hours.
- Serve and enjoy.

Calories 322, Fat 11.1 g, Carbohydrates 17.4 g, Sugar 2.4 g, Protein 36.9 g, Cholesterol 101 mg

Creamy Coconut Chicken Curry

Total Time: 4 hours 15 minutes

Serves:

4

- 1 lb chicken breasts, skinless and boneless
- 2 tbsp lemon juice
- 1 cup green peas
- 1/2 tsp cayenne
- 2 tbsp curry powder
- 15 oz can tomato sauce
- 1/2 cup chicken stock
- 1/2 cup coconut milk
- 2 medium sweet potatoes, diced
- 15 oz can chickpeas, drained and rinsed
- 1 medium onion, sliced
- 1 tsp salt

- Add all ingredients except peas into the slow cooker and mix well.
- Cover and cook on high for 4 hours.
- Add peas and stir well.
- Serve and enjoy.

Calories 579, Fat 17.9 g, Carbohydrates 62.4 g, Sugar 9.5 g, Protein 44.2 g, Cholesterol 101 mg

Tasty Chicken Kheema

Total Time: 4 hours 20 minutes

Serves:

4

- 1 lb ground chicken
- 3/4 cup frozen peas
- 1 bay leaf
- 3/4 tsp ground cinnamon
- 3/4 tsp garam masala
- 3/4 tsp ground turmeric
- 3/4 tsp chili powder
- 3/4 tsp ground cumin
- 3/4 tsp ground coriander
- 1 jalapeno, seeded and chopped
- 4 tbsp cilantro, chopped
- 3/4 cup can tomato sauce
- 1 tsp ginger, grated
- 3 garlic cloves, minced
- 1 medium onion, chopped
- 2 tsp butter
- 1 tsp kosher salt

- Heat butter in a pan over medium heat.
- Add onion to the pan and sauté for 5 minutes.
- Add ginger and garlic and sauté for 2 minutes.
- Add ground chicken and salt and cook for 5 minutes.
- Transfer chicken mixture to the slow cooker along with remaining ingredients and stir well.
- Cover and cook on high for 4 hours.
- Serve and enjoy.

Calories 291, Fat 10.8 g, Carbohydrates 11.8 g, Sugar 4.7 g, Protein 35.8 g, Cholesterol 106 mg

Shredded Lamb

Total Time: 6 hours 15 minutes

Serves:

6

4.4 lbs lamb shoulder

3 tsp vegetable oil

1 cup chicken stock

1 tbsp ginger, sliced

4 garlic cloves, crushed

2 large onions, sliced

Spice Rub:

1 tsp red chili powder

1 tsp ground coriander

6 peppercorns

1 tsp fennel seeds

1 bay leaf

1 tsp cumin seeds

1 cinnamon stick

6 cloves

1-star anise

- Add allspice rub ingredients into the grinder and grind to coarse powder.
- Rub spice powder onto the lamb from both the sides.
- Heat oil in the pan over medium-high heat.
- Place lamb onto the pan and brown them on both the sides and set aside.
- Add remaining ingredients into the slow cooker.
- Place lamb into the slow cooker.
- Cover and cook on high for 6 hours or until meat is tender.
- Remove lamb from slow cooker and using fork shred the meat.
- Return shredded meat to the slow cooker and stir well.
- Serve with rice and enjoy.

Calories 671, Fat 27.1 g, Carbohydrates 6.7 g, Sugar 2.3 g, Protein 94.4 g, Cholesterol 299 mg

Yummy Chicken Soup

Total Time: 12 hours 15 minutes

Serves: 6

- 3 carrots, peeled and sliced
- 1 tsp ginger, crushed
- 1/2 tsp garlic, crushed
- 1/4 tsp turmeric
- 1/2 onion, diced
- 12 cups water
- 5 cloves
- 2 cinnamon sticks
- 1/4 tsp black peppercorns
- 2 chicken breasts
- 1 lb chicken
- 1 tbsp sea salt

- Add all ingredients into the slow cooker.
- Cover and cook on low for 12 hours.
- Remove chicken from slow cooker and using fork shred the chicken.
- Return shredded chicken to the slow cooker and stir well.
- Season with pepper and salt.
- Serve and enjoy.

Calories 225, Fat 5.9 g, Carbohydrates 4.3 g, Sugar 1.9 g, Protein 36.4 g, Cholesterol 102 mg

LENTIL RECIPES

Healthy Lentil Curry

Total Time: 5 hours 10 minutes

Serves: 6

- 1 1/2 cups green lentils, rinse and drained
- 3 tbsp tomato paste
- 14 oz can coconut milk
- 3 tsp curry powder
- 1 onion, diced
- 3 garlic cloves, minced
- 1 yellow pepper, diced
- 1/4 tsp pepper
- 1/2 tsp ground ginger
- 2 tsp garam masala
- 2 tsp sugar
- 2 1/2 cups water
- 2 tbsp olive oil
- 1 tsp garlic powder
- 1 tsp cumin

1 1/2 tsp salt

- Add olive oil, yellow pepper, garlic, and onion into the slow cooker.
- Add lentils into the slow cooker and stir well.
- Add all remaining ingredients and stir well.
- Cover and cook on low for 5 hours.
- Stir well and serve with rice.

Calories 376, Fat 19 g, Carbohydrates 39 g, Sugar 4 g, Protein 15 g, Cholesterol 0 mg

Delicious Black Lentil Curry

Total Time: 12 hours 15 minutes

Serves: 8

- 1 cup whole black gram lentils
- 3 cloves
- 1 tbsp ginger, chopped
- 8 garlic cloves, chopped
- 2 green chilies, cut lengthwise
- 1 tbsp coriander powder
- 1/2 tsp turmeric powder
- 1/2 cup kidney beans
- 1 bay leaf
- 1 cinnamon stick
- 3 cardamom pods
- 1/2 tsp chili powder
- 4 tomatoes, diced
- 1 tsp garam masala
- 1/4 cup cream

2 tbsp butter

Salt

- Soak black lentils and kidney beans in water for overnight.
- Add all ingredients except cream into the slow cooker with 4 cups water and stir well.
- Cover and cook on low for 12 hours.
- Stir well and lightly mash using the back of a spoon.
- Add cream and stir well.
- Serve and enjoy.

Calories 186, Fat 4 g, Carbohydrates 27 g, Sugar 2 g, Protein 10 g, Cholesterol 9 mg

Lentil Butternut Squash Curry

Total Time: 12 hours 15 minutes

Serves: 8

- 2 cups red lentils
- 4 cups butternut squash, cut into cubes
- 2 tbsp ginger, minced
- 1 1/2 tsp curry powder
- 1 tsp ground coriander
- 1 onion, minced
- 2 garlic cloves, minced
- 1 tsp garam masala
- 1 tsp turmeric
- 14 oz can coconut milk
- 19 oz can tomatoes, diced
- 3 cups vegetable stock
- 1 tsp ground cumin
- 1/2 tsp salt

- Add all ingredients into the slow cooker and stir well.
- Cover and cook on low for 8 hours.
- Serve and enjoy.

Calories 329, Fat 11 g, Carbohydrates 45 g, Sugar 5 g, Protein 15 g, Cholesterol 0 mg

Simple Slow Cooker Lentil

Total Time: 6 hours 15 minutes

Serves: 6

- 2 cups red lentils, rinsed and drained
- 1 bay leaf
- 1 tbsp ground turmeric
- 1 tbsp fresh ginger, grated
- 1 medium onion, diced
- 15 oz can tomatoes, diced
- 5 cups water
- 1 tsp fennel seeds
- 2 tsp mustard seeds
- 2 tsp cumin seeds
- 1/4 tsp ground black pepper
- 1 tsp kosher salt

- Heat pan over medium heat and toast fennel seeds, mustard seeds, and cumin seeds in a pan until fragrant for 2-3 minutes.
- Add toasted spices and remaining all ingredients into the slow cooker and stir well.
- Cover and cook on low for 6 hours.
- Stir well and serve.

Calories 265, Fat 1 g, Carbohydrates 46 g, Sugar 4 g, Protein 18 g, Cholesterol 0 mg

Lentil Potato Coconut Curry

Total Time: 8 hours 15 minutes

Serves: 10

- 2 cups brown lentils
- 14 oz can coconut milk
- 3 cups vegetable broth
- 15 oz can tomato sauce
- 15 oz can tomatoes, diced
- 1/4 tsp ground cloves
- 3 tbsp curry powder
- 2 medium carrots, peel and diced
- 1 sweet potato, peel and diced
- 2 garlic cloves, minced
- 1 medium onion, diced

- Add all ingredients except coconut milk into the slow cooker and stir well.

- Cover and cook on low for 8 hours.
- Stir in coconut milk and serve with rice.

Calories 152, Fat 3 g, Carbohydrates 22 g, Sugar 6 g, Protein 9 g, Cholesterol 0 mg

Spicy Lentil Stew

Total Time: 6 hours 15 minutes

Serves: 8

3 cups red lentils, rinsed and drained

3 1/2 cup tomatoes, crushed

1/2 tbsp black pepper

1/2 tbsp curry powder

1/2 tbsp paprika

1/2 tbsp chili powder

1/2 tbsp garam masala

1/2 tbsp turmeric powder

6 cups vegetable broth

1 onion, diced

2 garlic cloves, minced

3 Serrano chili, diced

2 tbsp cilantro, minced

1 tbsp Creole seasoning

1 tbsp garlic powder

1 tbsp onion powder

1/2 tbsp ginger powder

- Add all ingredients into the slow cooker and stir well.
- Cover and cook on high for 5 hours.
- Uncover the slow cooker and cook for another 50 minutes.
- Serve and enjoy.

Calories 318, Fat 2 g, Carbohydrates 51 g, Sugar 5 g, Protein 23 g, Cholesterol 0 mg

Gluten Free Masala Lentils

Total Time: 6 hours 10 minutes

Serves: 8

- 2 1/4 cups brown lentils
- 4 cups vegetable broth
- 15 oz can tomatoes, diced
- 1 medium onion, chopped
- 3 garlic cloves, minced
- 1 tbsp fresh ginger, minced
- 1/4 cup tomato paste
- 2 tsp tamarind paste
- 1 tsp maple syrup
- 1 1/2 tsp garam masala
- 1 cup coconut milk
- 3/4 tsp salt

- Add all ingredients except coconut milk into the slow cooker and stir well.
- Cover and cook on low for 6 hours.
- Stir in coconut milk and serve.

Calories 306, Fat 9 g, Carbohydrates 41 g, Sugar 5 g, Protein 17 g, Cholesterol 0 mg

Flavorful Red Lentils Curry

Total Time: 8 hours 15 minutes

Serves: 16

4 cups brown lentils, rinsed and drained

5 tbsp red curry paste

1 tbsp garam masala

1 1/2 tsp turmeric

2 tsp sugar

1/2 cup coconut milk

29 oz can tomato puree

2 onions, diced

4 garlic cloves, minced

1 tbsp ginger, minced

4 tbsp butter

7 cups water

1 tsp salt

- Add all ingredients except coconut milk into the slow cooker and stir well.
- Cover and cook on low for 8 hours.
- Add coconut milk and stir well.
- Serve with rice and enjoy.

Calories 261, Fat 6 g, Carbohydrates 37 g, Sugar 4 g, Protein 13 g, Cholesterol 8 mg

Cauliflower Lentil Curry

Total Time: 5 hours 15 minutes

Serves: 6

- 1 cup red lentils
- 3 cups cauliflower, cut into florets
- 3 dates, pitted and chopped
- 2/3 cup coconut milk
- 1 1/2 tsp turmeric
- 1 tsp ginger, grated
- 2 tbsp Thai red curry paste
- 3 garlic cloves, minced
- 1/2 onion, chopped
- 3 cups vegetable broth
- 1/4 tsp sea salt

- Add all ingredients except coconut milk into the slow cooker and stir well.
- Cover and cook on low for 5 hours.
- Add coconut milk and stir well.

- Serve with rice and enjoy.

Calories 247, Fat 9 g, Carbohydrates 29 g, Sugar 6 g, Protein 12 g, Cholesterol 0 mg

Delicious Tempered Lentils

Total Time: 6 hours 20 minutes

Serves:

6

- 1 1/2 cups yellow split lentils, rinsed and drained
- 1/4 cup fresh cilantro, chopped
- 1 tsp turmeric powder
- 2 tsp garlic, minced
- 2 medium tomatoes, chopped
- 1/2 medium onion, chopped
- 1 tsp salt

For tempering:

- 2 tbsp vegetable oil
- 1/4 tsp chili powder
- 1/2 tsp coriander powder
- 1/2 tsp cumin powder
- 1 garlic cloves, minced
- 1/2 tsp whole cumin seeds

- Add lentils into the slow cooker with 4 cups water.

- Add turmeric powder, garlic, tomatoes, onion, and salt into the slow cooker and stir well.
- Cover and cook on low for 5 hours.
- Heat vegetable oil in the pan over medium-high heat.
- Once the oil is hot then turn off the heat and add cumin, garlic, and spices. Mix well.
- Stir prepared tempering into the hot lentil.
- Add cilantro and stir well.
- Cook lentils for another 1 hour to blend all flavors.
- Serve hot with rice and enjoy.

Calories 208, Fat 5.2 g, Carbohydrates 28 g, Sugar 1.5 g, Protein 12.7 g, Cholesterol 0 mg

Lentil Sweet Potato Soup

Total Time: 6 hours 20 minutes

Serves:

4

- 1 1/2 cups brown lentils
- 1 large sweet potato, cut into 1/2 inch cubes
- 6 cups vegetable broth
- 1 cup coconut milk
- 1/2 tbsp chili paste
- 1 medium onion, diced
- 3 garlic cloves, minced
- 1/2 tbsp ginger, grated
- 2 tsp ground cumin
- 1 tsp garam masala
- 2 tsp lime juice
- 1/4 cup fresh cilantro, chopped
- 14 oz can tomatoes, diced
- Pepper
- Salt

- Add all ingredients except tomatoes and lime juice into the slow cooker and stir well.
- Cover and cook on low for 6 hours.
- Stir in tomatoes and lime juice.
- Cook soup for another 10 minutes to blend the flavors.
- Season with pepper and salt.
- Serve warm and enjoy.

Calories 395, Fat 17 g, Carbohydrates 54 g, Sugar 11 g, Protein 23 g, Cholesterol 1 mg

Potato Red Lentil Curry

Total Time: 4 hours 15 minutes

Serves:

8

- 1 cup red lentils, rinsed
- 2 potatoes, cut into cubed
- 1 cup brown lentil, rinsed
- 1 large onion, diced
- 1/2 tsp turmeric
- 1/2 tsp cumin seeds, toasted
- 1 tsp sugar
- 14 oz can tomato, diced
- 14 oz can coconut milk
- 1 tbsp garlic, minced
- 1 tsp ginger, minced
- 2 tbsp butter
- 2 tbsp curry powder
- 1/2 tsp red pepper flakes

- Add all ingredients except coconut milk into the slow cooker and stir well.
- Add water into the slow cooker to cover lentil mixture.
- Cover and cook on high for 4 hours.
- Add coconut milk and stir well.
- Serve warm and enjoy.

Calories 307, Fat 14 g, Carbohydrates 39 g, Sugar 3 g, Protein 13 g, Cholesterol 8 mg

Healthy Spinach Lentils

Total Time: 4 hours 30 minutes

Serves:

4

---

1 cup yellow split peas

3 1/2 cups water

10 oz spinach, chopped

1 tsp cumin seeds

1 tbsp fresh ginger, peeled and minced

3 garlic cloves, minced

1 tsp mustard seeds

1 medium onion, diced

15 oz can tomatoes, drained and diced

2 jalapeno pepper, cored and diced

1 tsp turmeric

1/2 tsp coriander

1/4 tsp cayenne

1 tsp salt

- Add all ingredients except spinach into the slow cooker and stir well.
- Cover and cook on high for 4 hours.
- Add spinach and cook for another 20.
- Stir well and serve.

Calories 236, Fat 1.4 g, Carbohydrates 43 g, Sugar 9 g, Protein 16.1 g, Cholesterol 0 mg

Easy Lentils Rice

Total Time: 4 hours 10 minutes

Serves:

6

- 1/2 cup lentils, rinsed and drained
- 1 tsp garlic powder
- 3 1/2 cups vegetable broth
- 1 tbsp curry powder
- 1 cup white rice, rinsed and drained
- 1 onion, diced
- 1/4 tsp pepper
- Salt

- Add all ingredients into the slow cooker and stir well.
- Cover and cook on high for 4 hours.
- Stir well and serve.

Calories 204, Fat 1.3 g, Carbohydrates 37 g, Sugar 1.7 g, Protein 9.6 g, Cholesterol 0 mg

Lentil Chicken Vegetable Curry

Total Time: 4 hours 20 minutes

Serves:

8

- 1 lb dried lentils, rinsed and drained
- 4 cups fresh spinach, chopped
- 4 cups vegetable broth
- 1/4 tsp cinnamon
- 1 1/2 tsp turmeric
- 1/2 tsp cayenne
- 1 tbsp curry powder
- 2 lbs chicken thighs, boneless and cut into pieces
- 6 garlic cloves, minced
- 1 small cauliflower head, cut into florets
- 2 cups carrots, chopped
- 1 large onion, chopped
- 1 tsp salt

- Add all ingredients except spinach into the slow cooker and stir well.
- Cover and cook on high for 3 1/2 hours.
- Add spinach and stir well. Cover and cook for another 30 minutes.
- Stir well and serve with rice.

Calories 473, Fat 10 g, Carbohydrates 42 g, Sugar 4.6 g, Protein 51 g, Cholesterol 101 mg

Healthy Green Lentil Curry

Total Time: 6 hours 15 minutes

Serves:

6

- 2 cups green lentils, rinsed and drained
- 3 cups water
- 6 oz can tomato paste
- 14 oz can coconut milk
- 1 tsp cumin
- 1 tsp curry powder
- 1/2 tsp ground coriander
- 1 tsp turmeric
- 1 tsp vegetable oil
- 6 garlic cloves, minced
- 1 large onion, chopped
- 1 1/4 tsp salt

- Heat oil in the pan over medium heat.
- Add garlic and onion to the pan and sauté for 5 minutes.
- Add cumin, curry powder, coriander, turmeric, and salt and sauté for 1 minute.
- Transfer pan mixture to the slow cooker with remaining all ingredients. Stir well.
- Cover and cook on low for 6 hours.
- Serve warm with rice and enjoy.

Calories 404, Fat 15.9 g, Carbohydrates 49 g, Sugar 5.9 g, Protein 19.7 g, Cholesterol 0 mg

Smokey Lentil Soup

Total Time: 6 hours 15 minutes

Serves:

6

- 2 cups red lentils
- 2 tbsp smoked paprika
- 2 carrots, chopped
- 4 garlic cloves, minced
- 8 cups vegetable broth
- 1 onion, chopped
- 3 tbsp fresh parsley, chopped
- 1/4 cup hulled pumpkin seeds
- 2 potatoes, peeled and chopped
- 1/3 cup tomato paste
- 3 tbsp lemon juice
- 3 tbsp vegetable oil

- Add lentils, lemon juice, tomato paste, garlic, paprika, carrots, potato, onion, and broth into the slow cooker and stir well.
- Cover and cook on low for 6 hours.
- Meanwhile, in a small bowl, combine together parsley and oil.
- Ladle soup into the bowls and drizzle with parsley and oil mixture.
- Sprinkle pumpkin seeds over the soup.
- Serve and enjoy.

Calories 474, Fat 9.9 g, Carbohydrates 67.6 g, Sugar 7 g, Protein 25.8 g, Cholesterol 0 mg

Spinach Coconut Lentil Soup

Total Time: 4 hours 45 minutes

Serves:

6

---

4 cups fresh spinach, chopped

14 oz coconut milk

4 cups vegetable stock

1 1/2 cup red lentils, rinsed and drained

1 tsp ground cinnamon

1/2 tsp garam masala

1 tsp ground turmeric

1 tsp ground coriander seed

1 tsp ground cumin

2 tsp garlic, minced

1 large onion, chopped

1 tbsp vegetable oil

Pepper

Salt

- Heat oil in the pan over medium heat.
- Add onion to the pan and sauté for 5 minutes or until golden brown.
- Add cinnamon, garam masala, turmeric, coriander, cumin, and garlic and cook for 2 minutes.
- Transfer onion-spice mixture into the slow cooker.
- Add lentils and stock into the slow cooker and stir well.
- Cover and cook on low for 4 hours.
- Add coconut milk and spinach. Stir well and cook for another 30 minutes.
- Season with pepper and salt.
- Serve and enjoy.

Calories 368, Fat 20 g, Carbohydrates 37 g, Sugar 5 g, Protein 14.9 g, Cholesterol 0 mg

Spicy Keema Lentils

Total Time: 4 hours 15 minutes

Serves: 4

- 3 cups green lentils, cooked
- 1 tsp dried chili flakes
- 1/2 tsp ground turmeric
- 2 tsp garam masala
- 2 tsp ground coriander
- 2 tsp ground cumin
- 1 large onion, chopped
- 3 tbsp fresh ginger, grated
- 6 garlic cloves, chopped
- 1 1/2 cup vegetable broth
- 2 tbsp tamari
- 1 tsp pepper
- 1 tsp salt

- Add all ingredients into the slow cooker and stir well.
- Cover and cook on low for 4 hours.
- Stir well and serve.

Calories 206, Fat 0.9 g, Carbohydrates 37 g, Sugar 2 g Protein 15 g, Cholesterol 0 mg

Creamy Split Pea Curry

Total Time: 6 hours 15 minutes

Serves:

6

- 1 1/2 cups dried split peas
- 1 cup heavy cream
- 1/2 tsp ground ginger
- 2 tsp curry powder
- 1 tbsp turmeric
- 1 tbsp green curry paste
- 3 garlic cloves, minced
- 1/2 cup onion, diced
- 15 oz can coconut milk
- 28 oz can tomatoes, crushed
- 1 tsp salt

- Add all ingredients except cream into the slow cooker. Stir well.
- Cover and cook on low for 6 hours.
- Add cream and stir well.
- Serve with rice and enjoy.

Calories 425, Fat 23.8 g, Carbohydrates 42.4 g, Sugar 9 g, Protein 15.5 g, Cholesterol 27 mg

Lentil Vegetable Soup

Total Time: 8 hours 15 minutes

Serves:

8

- 1 1/2 cups green lentils, rinsed and drained
- 9 cups vegetable broth
- 5 peppercorns
- 3 bay leaves
- 3 tbsp soy sauce
- 1 tsp thyme
- 2 tsp oregano
- 1 tbsp garlic powder
- 2 cups corn
- 4 cups potatoes, diced
- 3 large carrots, diced
- 3 large celery stalks, diced
- 2 medium onion, diced

- Add all ingredients into the slow cooker and mix well.
- Cover and cook on low for 8 hours.
- Discard peppercorns and bay leaves from soup and using blender puree the soup until you get desired texture.
- Serve hot and enjoy.

Calories 288, Fat 2.6 g, Carbohydrates 49 g, Sugar 6.7 g, Protein 18.5 g, Cholesterol 0 mg

Delicious Lemon Lentils

Total Time: 2 hours 45 minutes

Serves:

8

- 1 1/2 cups pink lentils
- 1 tbsp milk
- 2 tbsp lemon juice
- 2 Serrano chilies, sliced
- 1 tbsp fresh ginger, minced
- 4 garlic cloves, sliced
- 1 small onion, diced
- 5 cups water
- 1 1/2 tsp salt

- Add all ingredients except milk and lemon juice into the slow cooker. Stir well.
- Cover and cook on high for 2 1/2 hours.
- Add lemon juice and stir well.
- Add milk and stir well and serve.

Calories 135, Fat 0.9 g, Carbohydrates 23.4 g, Sugar 0.6 g, Protein 9.4 g, Cholesterol 0 mg

Tasty Carrot Lentils Soup

Total Time: 8 hours 15 minutes

Serves:

8

1/2 cup lentils

2 lbs carrots, peeled and cut into 1-inch pieces

1/2 tsp harissa

1/4 cup maple syrup

1 cup orange juice

4 cups vegetable broth

1 tsp fresh ginger, grated

1/2 tbsp ground cumin

1/2 tbsp curry powder

1 medium onion, peeled and chopped

Pepper

Salt

- Add orange juice, broth, ginger, curry powder, onion, and carrots into the slow cooker and mix well.
- Cover and cook on low for 6 hours.
- Add lentils, harissa, and maple syrup. Stir well and cook on high for another 2 hours.
- Season with pepper and salt.
- Serve and enjoy.

Calories 158, Fat 1.1 g, Carbohydrates 30.6 g Sugar 15.3 g Protein 7 g, Cholesterol 0 mg

Lentil Sweet Potato Beans Stew

Total Time: 6 hours 30 minutes

Serves:

6

- 3/4 cup dry lentils, rinsed and drained
- 3 cups sweet potatoes, cut into 1 inch cubed
- 1 1/2 cups green beans, cut into pieces
- 1 1/2 cups baby carrots
- 1/2 cup plain yogurt
- 1 3/4 cup vegetable broth
- 2 garlic cloves, minced
- 1 tsp fresh ginger, chopped
- 1 tsp ground cumin
- 1 tbsp curry powder
- 2 tbsp vegetable oil
- 1/4 cup onion, chopped
- 1/4 tsp black pepper
- 1/2 tsp salt

- Add lentils, carrots, onion, and sweet potatoes into the slow cooker.
- In a pan, heat oil over medium heat.
- Add garlic, ginger, pepper, cumin, curry powder, and salt and stir for 1 minute. Stir in broth.
- Pour mixture into the slow cooker and mix well.
- Cover and cook on low for 6 hours.
- Turn heat to high and stir in green beans. Cover and cook for another 15 minutes.
- Top with plain yogurt and serve.

Calories 269, Fat 5.9 g, Carbohydrates 43.5 g, Sugar 4.8 g, Protein 10.8 g, Cholesterol 1 mg

BEANS AND PEAS RECIPES

Healthy Chickpeas and Tofu

Total Time: 4 hours 15 minutes

Serves:

6

- 12 oz firm tofu
- 15 oz can chickpeas, rinsed and drained
- 1/8 cup cilantro, chopped
- 1/2 tsp ground ginger
- 2 tsp chili powder
- 1 tbsp curry powder
- 1 tbsp garam masala
- 1 cup tomato puree
- 14 oz can coconut milk
- 4 garlic cloves, minced
- 1 medium onion, diced
- 1 tsp vegetable oil
- Pepper
- Salt

- Rinse tofu well and pat dry with paper towel. Squeeze out all liquid from tofu and cut tofu into the pieces.
- Heat oil in the saucepan over medium heat.
- Add onion to the pan and sauté for 5 minutes.
- Add garlic and cook for 1 minute.
- Whisk in coconut milk, ginger, chili powder, curry powder, garam masala, tomato puree, pepper, and salt. Cook for 5 minutes.
- Add chickpeas and tofu into the slow cooker.
- Pour pan mixture into the slow cooker.
- Cover and cook on low for 4 hours.
- Garnish with cilantro and serve.

Calories 294, Fat 18.5 g, Carbohydrates 26.2 g, Sugar 3.3 g, Protein 10.8 g, Cholesterol 0 mg

Chickpea Pumpkin Lentil Curry

Total Time: 8 hours 40 minutes

Serves:

6

- 15 oz can chickpeas, rinsed and drained
- 1 cup pumpkin puree
- 1 cup lentils, rinsed and drained
- 15 oz can coconut milk
- 1/4 tsp ground cayenne pepper
- 1 tbsp curry powder
- 2 cups vegetable broth
- 2 garlic cloves, minced
- 1 medium onion, diced
- 1 tsp kosher salt

- Add all ingredients except coconut milk into the slow cooker and stir well.
- Cover and cook on low for 8 hours.
- Add coconut milk and stir well. Cook for another 30 minutes.
- Serve with rice and enjoy.

Calories 376, Fat 17 g, Carbohydrates 43.5 g, Sugar 3.1 g, Protein 15.7 g, Cholesterol 0 mg

North Indian red Beans

Total Time: 4 hours 15 minutes

Serves:

4

- 2 cups dry red beans, soak for overnight
- 2 tbsp cilantro, chopped
- 1 cup tomato sauce
- 1 cinnamon stick
- 1/4 tsp turmeric
- 1/4 tsp cayenne pepper
- 1/4 tsp ground coriander
- 1 tbsp lemon juice
- 4 garlic cloves, minced
- 1 tsp ginger, minced
- 1 medium onion, chopped
- 1 tsp cumin seeds
- 1 bay leaf

1 tbsp vegetable oil

1 1/2 tsp salt

- Heat oil in the pan over medium heat.
- Add onion, bay leaf, and cumin seeds into the pan and cook for 5 minutes.
- Add dry spices and lemon juice and stir for 2 minutes.
- Add beans, cinnamon stick, tomato sauce, and salt into the slow cooker.
- Transfer pan mixture into the slow cooker and stir well.
- Cover and cook on high for 4 hours.
- Using spoon lightly mash the red beans it helps to thicken the gravy.
- Garnish with cilantro and serve.

Calories 376, Fat 4.8 g, Carbohydrates 64.1 g, Sugar 5.9 g, Protein 22.2 g, Cholesterol 0 mg

Simple Black Eyed Peas

Total Time: 6 hours 15 minutes

Serves:

6

- 1 lb dried black-eyed peas, soak for overnight
- 1 tsp ground sage
- 1/8 tsp thyme
- 1 bay leaf
- 1 garlic clove, diced
- 1 small onion, diced
- 2 cups water
- 2 cups vegetable broth
- 1/2 tsp pepper
- 1 tsp sea salt

- Add all ingredients into the slow cooker and mix well.
- Cover and cook on low for 6 hours.
- Serve and enjoy.

Calories 203,nFat 0.5 g, Carbohydrates 48.8 g, Sugar 2.8 g, Protein 20.2 g, Cholesterol 0 mg

Tasty Black Eyed Pea Curry

Total Time: 4 hours 15 minutes

Serves:

4

- 1 cup dried black-eyed peas, soaked for overnight
- 1 bay leaf
- 6 garlic cloves, minced
- 1/2 tsp black pepper
- 1/4 tsp cayenne
- 2 tomatoes, chopped
- 3 cups water
- 1 tsp ginger, minced
- 1 tsp turmeric
- 1/2 tsp cumin seeds
- 1 large onion, diced
- 1 tsp garam masala
- 1 tsp salt

- Add all ingredients into the slow cooker and stir well.
- Cover and cook on high for 4 hours.
- Stir well and serve.

Calories 128, Fat 0.4 g, Carbohydrates 31.4 g, Sugar 4.3 g, Protein 10.4 gCholesterol 0 mg

Healthy Green Pea and Cauliflower Korma

Total Time: 4 hours 15 minutes

Serves:

4

- 10 oz green peas
- 1 cauliflower head, cut into florets
- 1 cup water
- 1 1/2 cups coconut milk
- 1/4 tsp cayenne
- 1 tsp turmeric
- 1/4 tsp cumin
- 2 tsp garam masala
- 1 medium onion, diced

- Add all ingredients into the slow cooker and stir well.
- Cover and cook on low for 4 hours.
- Stir well and serve.

Calories 295, Fat 21.9 g, Carbohydrates 21.8 g, Sugar 9.8 g, Protein 7.6 g, Cholesterol 0 mg

Red Beans Bowl

Total Time: 8 hours 15 minutes

Serves:

4

- 14 oz can kidney beans, drained and rinsed
- 1/2 tsp garam Masala
- 1/2 tsp turmeric powder
- 2 cups onion, chopped
- 1 tomato, chopped
- 1/2 inch cinnamon stick
- 1 bay leaf
- 2 cloves
- 1 tsp ginger, minced
- 5 garlic cloves, minced
- 1 green chili, chopped
- 1/2 tbsp cumin seeds
- 1 tsp cayenne pepper
- 1 tbsp paprika
- Salt

- Add all ingredients except yogurt into the slow cooker and stir well.
- Add 4 cups water and stir to combine.
- Cover and cook on high for 8 hours.
- Using back of spoon mash few beans.
- Stir well and serve with rice.

Calories 399, Fat 2.1 g, Carbohydrates 72.2 g, Sugar 7.4 g, Protein 25.6 g, Cholesterol 2 mg

Chickpea Lentil Chili

Total Time: 8 hours 15 minutes

Serves:

6

1 cup dried chickpeas, soaked overnight

1/2 cup raisins

2 1/2 cups vegetable broth

1/2 cup water

28 oz can whole tomatoes, undrained and crushed

2 cups sweet potatoes, cut into cubes

1 cup lentils

1/2 tsp chili powder

1/2 tsp ground cinnamon

1/4 tsp ground turmeric

1 cup onion, chopped

5 garlic cloves, minced

1 1/2 tsp ground cumin

1 tsp kosher salt

- Add all ingredients into the slow cooker and stir well.
- Cover and cook on low for 8 hours.
- Stir well and serve.

Calories 388, Fat 3.3 g, Carbohydrates 73.3 g, Sugar 17.3 g, Protein 19.6 g, Cholesterol 0 mg

Red Beans and Lentils

Total Time: 4 hours 15 minutes

Serves:

10

- 3 cups red beans, cooked
- 1 cup black lentils, rinsed and drained
- 1/4 tsp ground mustard
- 1/4 tsp ground nutmeg
- 1 tsp ground turmeric
- 1 tsp ground cardamom
- 1 1/2 tsp chili powder
- 3 tsp ground cumin
- 2 tbsp ginger, grated
- 6 garlic cloves, minced
- 5 cups water

For serving:

- 1 tsp garam masala
- 2 tsp ginger, grated
- 2 tsp tomato paste
- 1/2 cup cashew creamer
- Salt

- Add all ingredients except serving ingredients into the slow cooker and stir well.
- Cover and cook on high for 4 hours.
- Add all serving ingredients and stir well.
- Serve with rice and enjoy.

Calories 288, Fat 2.8 g, Carbohydrates 49.1 g, Sugar 2 g, Protein 18.4 g, Cholesterol 0 mg

Simple Chickpea Curry

Total Time: 6 hours 10 minutes

Serves:

6

- 15 oz can chickpeas
- 15 oz can coconut milk
- 15 oz can tomatoes, diced
- 1/4 tbsp cilantro, chopped
- 2 tbsp curry powder
- 1 tsp ginger, minced
- 4 garlic cloves, minced
- 2 onions, diced
- Salt

- Add all ingredients except cilantro into the slow cooker and stir well.
- Cover and cook on low for 6 hours.
- Garnish with cilantro and serve.

Calories 265, Fat 16.3 g, Carbohydrates 27.1 g, Sugar 4.1 g, Protein 6.4 g, Cholesterol 0 mg

Pea Chickpea Vegetable Curry

Total Time: 2 hours 15 minutes

Serves:

8

- 1 cup can chickpeas, drained
- 1 cup green peas
- 1 tsp red pepper flakes
- 1 tsp ground coriander
- 1 tsp ginger powder
- 2 tbsp curry powder
- 15 oz can coconut milk
- 2 cups vegetable broth
- 1 medium onion, diced
- 3/4 cup carrot, diced
- 1 1/2 cups potatoes, chopped
- 2 tsp sea salt

- Add all ingredients into the slow cooker and stir well.
- Cover and cook on high for 2 hours.
- Stir well and serve.

Calories 201, Fat 12.4 g, Carbohydrates 19 g, Sugar 2.7 g, Protein 5.7 g, Cholesterol 0 mg

Perfect Curried Baked Beans

Total Time: 8 hours 10 minutes

Serves:

8

- 4 cups pinto beans, cooked
- 1 tbsp vegetable oil
- 1 medium onion, diced
- 14 oz can coconut milk
- 6 oz can tomato paste
- 2 tbsp brown sugar
- 1 garlic cloves, minced
- 1 tbsp fresh ginger, minced
- 3 tsp curry powder
- 1/8 tsp red pepper flakes
- 1/2 tsp cumin
- 1/2 tsp salt

- Add cooked beans into the slow cooker.
- Heat oil in the pan over medium heat.
- Add onion and sauté for 5 minutes.
- Add garlic and sauté for another 1 minute.
- Stir in crushed red peppers, cumin, curry powder, ginger, and salt.
- Reduce heat and stir in coconut milk, brown sugar, and tomato paste.
- Pour pan mixture over the beans and stir well.
- Cover slow cooker and cook on low for 8 hours.
- Serve and enjoy.

Calories 485, Fat 13 g, Carbohydrates 70.4 g, Sugar 7.4 g, Protein 22.9 g, Cholesterol 0 mg

Red Beans with Bell Pepper

Total Time: 5 hours 10 minutes

Serves:

4

- 3/4 cup celery, chopped
- 1 tsp dried thyme
- 1 tsp paprika
- 3/4 tsp ground red pepper
- 1/2 tsp ground black pepper
- 3 cups water
- 1 cup dried red beans
- 1 cup onion, chopped
- 1 cup green bell pepper, chopped
- 14 oz turkey sausage, sliced
- 1 bay leaf
- 5 garlic cloves, minced
- 1/2 tsp salt

- Add all ingredients into the slow cooker and stir well.
- Cover and cook on high for 5 hours.
- Stir well and serve with rice.

Calories 525, Fat 29 g, Carbohydrates 35.8 g, Sugar 4.1 g, Protein 30.8 g, Cholesterol 83 mg

Spicy Black Eyed Peas

Total Time: 6 hours 30 minutes

Serves:

10

- 1 lb dried black-eyed peas, rinsed and drained
- 1 tsp ground black pepper
- 1 1/2 tsp cumin
- 1/2 tsp cayenne pepper
- 1 jalapeno pepper, seeded and minced
- 1 red bell pepper, seeded and diced
- 2 garlic cloves, diced
- 1 onion, diced
- 6 cups water
- Salt

- Add all ingredients into the slow cooker and stir well.
- Cover and cook on low for 6 hours.
- Serve and enjoy.

Calories 122, Fat 0.2 g, Carbohydrates 30.7 g, Sugar 2.4 g, Protein 11.4 g, Cholesterol 0 mg

Chickpea Coconut Quinoa Curry

Total Time: 4 hours 20 minutes

Serves:

8

- 3 cups sweet potato, peeled and cut into cubes
- 2 cups broccoli florets
- 14.5 oz can coconut milk
- 1/4 cup quinoa
- 2 garlic cloves, minced
- 1 tbsp ginger, grated
- 1 cup onion, diced
- 15 oz can chickpeas, drained and rinsed
- 28 oz can tomatoes, diced
- 1 tsp ground turmeric
- 2 tsp tamari
- 1 tsp chili flakes

- Add all ingredients into the slow cooker and stir well.
- Cover and cook on high for 4 hours.
- Serve and enjoy.

Calories 291, Fat 12.2 g, Carbohydrates 41.3 g, Sugar 9.3 g, Protein 7.9 g, Cholesterol 0 mg

Red Beans Cabbage Soup

Total Time: 8 hours 10 minutes

Serves:

6

- 15 oz can red beans, drained and rinsed
- 4 cups water
- 4 garlic cloves, minced
- 1 bay leaf
- 1 tsp dried thyme
- 5 oz can tomato paste
- 1/2 head green cabbage, chopped
- 1 green bell pepper, seeded and diced
- 1 medium onion, diced
- 1 medium carrots, peeled and diced
- 1/4 tsp black pepper
- Salt

- Add all ingredients into the slow cooker and stir well.
- Cover and cook on high for 8 hours.
- Stir well and serve.

Calories 275, Fat 0.9 g, Carbohydrates 51.9 g, Sugar 8.6 g, Protein 18.4 g, Cholesterol 0 mg

Gluten Free Chickpea Curry

Total Time: 4 hours 10 minutes

Serves:

4

- 14 oz can chickpeas, drained
- 3 cup sweet potatoes, peeled and chopped
- 1/2 tsp chili flakes
- 1 tbsp honey
- 1 tsp ground cumin
- 2 tsp ground turmeric
- 2 tsp garam masala
- 13 oz can cream
- 1 tsp vegetable oil
- 1 tbsp fresh ginger, grated
- 4 garlic cloves, minced
- 1 large onion, chopped

- Heat oil in the pan over medium heat.
- Add onion, garlic, and ginger to the pan and sauté for 5 minutes.
- Add onion mixture into the blender along with honey, spices, cream, and salt and blend until smooth.
- Add remaining ingredients and curry blend into the slow cooker and stir well.
- Cover and cook on high for 4 hours.
- Serve and enjoy.

Calories 636, Fat 17.9 g, Carbohydrates 113.6 g, Sugar 54.1 g, Protein 8.7 g, Cholesterol 0 mg

Vegetarian Chili Bowl

Total Time: 4 hours 20 minutes

Serves:

8

- 1 tsp garam masala
- 4 large tomatoes, peeled, seeded and chopped
- 1/3 cup can black beans, drained and rinsed
- 1/3 cup can chickpea, rinsed and drained
- 1 1/2 cups onions, chopped
- 1 cup green bell peppers, chopped
- 3 garlic cloves, minced
- 1/3 cup can red beans, rinsed and drained
- 1 1/2 cup vegetable stock
- 2 tbsp fresh cilantro, chopped
- 2 tbsp vegetable oil
- 2 green chili, minced
- 1/2 medium zucchini, cut into pieces
- 1 cup celery, chopped
- 1/2 tbsp chili powder
- 1/2 tbsp ground coriander
- 1/2 tsp cumin powder

1 tsp dried oregano

1 tsp dried thyme

1 tsp fresh ginger

1/4 tsp turmeric

1 1/4 tsp salt

- Heat oil in the pan over medium heat.
- Add onion, celery, green chilies, and ginger into the pan and sauté for 5 minutes.
- Add spices and stir for another 2 minutes.
- Add remaining all ingredients into the slow cooker along with pan mixture. stir well.
- Cover and cook on low for 8 hours.
- Serve and enjoy.

Calories 135, Fat 5.7 g, Carbohydrates 19.5 g, Sugar 6.7 g, Protein 4.4 g, Cholesterol 0 mg

Healthy Turmeric Lentil Bean Chili

Total Time: 4 hours 15 minutes

Serves:

6

- 15 oz can red beans, rinsed and drained
- 1 cup coconut milk
- 1 tsp turmeric
- 1 tsp chili powder
- 1 tsp ground cumin
- 6 oz can tomato paste
- 2 cups water
- 32 oz vegetable stock
- 1 small onion, chopped
- 2 cups green lentils, rinsed and drained

- Add all ingredients except coconut milk into the slow cooker and stir well.
- Cover and cook on high for 4 hours.
- Add coconut milk and stir well.

- Stir well and serve.

Calories 598, Fat 11.5 g, Carbohydrates 92.6 g, Sugar 9.2 g, Protein 35.5 g, Cholesterol 0 mg

Chickpea Kale Sweet Potato Stew

Total Time: 4 hours 20 minutes

Serves:

8

- 15.5 oz can chickpeas, drained and rinsed
- 5 oz kale, chopped
- 2 red bell peppers, diced
- 1 1/2 lbs sweet potatoes, peeled and cut into pieces
- 2 tbsp curry powder
- 1 tsp fresh ginger, peeled and minced
- 3 garlic cloves, minced
- 2 cups vegetable broth
- 14.5 oz can tomatoes, drained and diced
- 1/4 tsp black pepper
- 14 oz can coconut milk
- 1 tsp vegetable oil
- 1 large onion, diced
- 1 tbsp kosher salt

- Heat oil in the pan over medium heat.

- Add onion and 1 tsp salt and sauté for 5 minutes.
- Add potatoes and 1 tsp salt and sauté for another 5 minutes.
- Add curry powder, garlic, and ginger and stir for 2 minutes.
- Add pan mixture into the slow cooker along with remaining ingredients except for kale and coconut milk.
- Cover and cook on high for 4 hours.
- Add coconut milk and kale and stir well. Cook for another 10 minutes.
- Serve and enjoy.

Calories 323, Fat 12.6 g, Carbohydrates 47.7 g, Sugar 4.7 g, Protein 8 g, Cholesterol 0 mg

Chickpea Spinach Cauliflower Curry

Total Time: 6 hours 15 minutes

Serves:

6

- 2 cups baby spinach, chopped
- 15 oz can chickpeas
- 1/2 tbsp curry powder
- 1 tbsp garam masala
- 1 cup vegetable broth
- 14 oz can coconut milk
- 1 sweet potato, peeled and diced
- 2 cups cauliflower florets
- 2 cups can tomatoes, chopped
- 1 tbsp ginger, minced
- 1 garlic clove, minced
- 1/2 onion, chopped
- 1 tsp vegetable oil

1 tsp salt

- Heat oil in the pan over medium heat.
- Add ginger, garlic, and onion to the pan and sauté for 5 minutes.
- Add pan mixture into the slow cooker with remaining ingredients except for spinach.
- Cover and cook on low for 6 hours.
- Add spinach and stir well.
- Serve with rice and enjoy.

Calories 282, Fat 16.1 g, Carbohydrates 30.1 g, Sugar 5.3 g, Protein 8 g, Cholesterol 0 mg

Spicy Winter Chickpeas

Total Time: 6 hours 15 minutes

Serves:

4

- 1 1/2 cups dried chickpeas, rinsed and drained
- 2 tbsp parsley, chopped
- 1 tbsp lemon juice
- 1 bay leaf
- 1/2 butternut squash, cut into 1-inch cubes
- 10 green olive, pitted
- 1 tsp tamarind paste
- 2 garlic cloves, minced
- 2 tomatoes, diced
- 1 large onion, chopped
- 2 tbsp vegetable oil
- 1/2 tsp ground black pepper
- 1 tsp curry powder
- 1 tsp ground ginger
- 1 tsp garam masala

1 tsp smoked paprika

1 tsp turmeric

1/2 tsp salt

- Heat oil in the pan over medium heat.
- Add garlic, ginger, and onion to the pan and sauté for 5 minutes.
- Add spices and sauté for 1 minute. Transfer mixture into the slow cooker.
- Add remaining ingredients into the slow cooker and stir well.
- Cover and cook on low for 6 hours.
- Serve and enjoy.

Calories 425, Fat 14.3 g, Carbohydrates 60.5 g, Sugar 12.6 g, Protein 16.3 g, Cholesterol 0 mg

Mixed Vegetable Raita

Serves 4

Ingredients

1 large potato, finely diced and boiled
25g/scant 1oz French beans, finely diced and boiled
25g/scant 1oz carrots, finely diced and boiled
50g/1¾oz boiled peas
450g/1lb yoghurt
½ tsp ground black pepper
1 tbsp coriander leaves, finely chopped
Salt to taste

Method

- Mix all the ingredients well in a bowl. Serve chilled.

Boondi Raita

Serves 4

Ingredients

115g/4oz salted boondi*
450g/1lb yoghurt
½ tsp sugar
½ tsp chaat masala*

Method

- Mix all the ingredients well in a bowl. Serve chilled.

Cauliflower Raita

Serves 4

Ingredients

250g/9oz cauliflower, chopped into tiny florets, or grated
Salt to taste
½ tsp ground black pepper
½ tsp chilli powder
½ tsp ground mustard
450g/1lb yoghurt
1 tsp ghee
½ tsp mustard seeds
Chaat masala* to taste

Method

- Mix the cauliflower with salt and steam mixture.
- Whisk the pepper, chilli powder, mustard, salt and yoghurt in a bowl.
- Add the cauliflower mixture to the yoghurt mixture and set aside.
- Heat the ghee in a small saucepan. When it begins to smoke, add the mustard seeds. Let them splutter for 15 seconds.
- Add this with the chaat masala to the yoghurt mixture. Serve chilled.